Forty-
Fabulous Funnies

and fourteen more for free!

Poems

by

STEVE HERBERT

Copyright © 2021 Steve Herbert

All rights reserved.

ISBN: 978-1-7957-8263-0

DEDICATION

To all those who have inspired me with humorous verse beyond compare.
I'll name a few, but sadly will have forgotten so many more.

Banjo Patterson, Robert Service, Lewis Carroll, Dr Seuss, Hilaire Belloc,
Pam Ayres, Ogden Nash, Shel Silverstein, Leunig, Marriott Edgar, Roger
McGough, Rudyard Kipling, everyone in *Verse and Worse*, and of course, the
greatest of them all, Mr, Mrs and Ms Anon (who uses no pronouns at all!)

ACKNOWLEDGMENTS

Once again I have to thank my enormously talented better half, not only for
putting up with my often unamusing musings and inane singsongs, but also
for creating the cover. Catch some of her digital creations as Figberrie
Bumblebrum on Facebook

If I had half of her artistic skill, I would have attempted to illustrate these
poems myself. They deserve the same visual quirkiness and humour
contained in the words. Lacking that, I have resorted to scouring the
internet for free images to do the job. The great majority of them come
from clker.com and Pixabay.com. The remainder came via a Google image
search and were labelled as copyright-free.

I also bestow a nod to my friends and fellow writers from the Kaipwriters
writing group. You know who you are.

CONTENTS

CAUTIONARY TALES

Ever since men first started telling stories, they have used them to warn others of danger and teach them the 'right' way to do things. In their earliest versions, traditional tales such as Little Red Riding Hood were simply horror stories aimed at young children to terrify them into obedience!

Much, much, much later, writers chose to make fun of these moralistic tales, satirising them by exaggerating how minor infractions could lead to the most grisly of consequences. The man most often credited with this gloriously humorous piss-taking is the very English writer with the very French name, Hilaire Belloc, who thrilled Victorian readers with such creations as "Matilda, Who Told Lies and Was Burned to Death" and "Jim, Who Ran Away From His Nurse and Was Eaten by a Lion," which provides us with the immortal lines:

Now just imagine how it feels
When first your toes and then your heels,
And then by gradual degrees,
Your shins and ankles, calves and knees,
Are slowly eaten, bit by bit.
No wonder Jim detested it."

This section contains eight of my own Cautionaries, some more gruesome than others!

KayCee
… who grew far too fond of mobile phones and met a dreadful fate

Here we go, channelling Hilaire Belloc – updated to the 21st Century, of course. Hang on, it's going to be quite a ride!

A girl named KayCee Forsyte-Jones
Grew far too fond of mobile phones.
There were a dozen she could choose
Of richly variegated hues -
A pink one with HDTV,
A green one that would help her pee
By imitating running water,
(Have you tried that? Perhaps you oughtta!)
A blue for music, red for school,
A purple one that, as a rule,
Young KayCee took to bed at night,
Although she knew it wasn't right,
For you, by now, should understand
That KayCee liked to have on hand
At least two phones and often three
So she could Tik-Tok, text (or pee)
At any time of night or day.
If she were yours, what would you say?

Her father, QC Rupert Jones,
Was not a fan of mobile phones.
"*IMHO,*" he gruffly said,
"*Don't hold that thing so near your head.
Invisible and deadly rays
May fill your brain with toxic sprays
And make a mishy-mushy splatter
Of what we used to call grey matter.*"

Her mother (She's the Forsyte part)
Told KayCee fondly from her heart,
"*Don't mind your father, KayCee dear,
That last case turned him rather queer,*

2

But really it would please us so
If just for once you would let go
Your phone while sitting at the table
And in the bath if you are able.
I have it on quite good advice
It isn't proper, isn't nice
To text while you are on the loo
Or while your boyfriend's kissing you."

Now KayCee (you may well have guessed)
Was in her teenage years, the best
Time of her life, so some would say,
(Though not her parents who've gone grey)
And teenagers, I'm sure you know,
Don't listen to their parents, so
Young KayCee shut out every word,
She thought it silly, quite absurd.
And then, another teenage trait,
She used her phone for six hours straight
And even when she went to bed
She clasped the thing tight to her head.
Oh, woe is me, the angels weep;
Miss Forsyte-Jones went off to sleep,
Her phone still plastered to one ear.
O, gentle reader, shed a tear,
For we all know that such offending
Just cannot have a happy ending.

Yes, overnight, as you suspected,
KayCee and her phone connected.
Now that is not a metaphor;
Though KayCee cried and scratched and swore
A flood, a torrent of abuse,
The wretched thing would not come loose.
In fact, by gradual degrees,
As KayCee shouted, *"Help me, please!"*
The purple phone oozed through her ear
Where it would fully disappear.
Quite gone! It vanished! Not a trace!
Except her slightly swollen face

And faintly, just the strangest thing,
Inside the girl there came a ring.

Now, Mrs Forsyte, Mr Jones,
Alerted by their daughter's tones,
Came racing to her urgent aid.
Alas, too late, for there, displayed
In KayCee's eyes, a message read,
"There's six missed calls. My battery's dead."

So to the hospital they rode,
Quite thankful for her silent mode,
And there the doctor, Ram Patel,
Cried, *"Oh, good gracious! Bloody Hell!"*
(He'd just arrived from Bangalore
Where evidently doctors swore)
"You know that this is nothing new;
I've seen such cases, quite a few.
She'll be OK, she's in no pain,
The phone's attaching to her brain.
The MRI shows that a probe
Is piercing her frontal lobe
And in medulla oblongata
Has started hijacking her data --
Miley Cyrus, favourite dolls,
Justin Bieber, fear of trolls --
In just an instant, I am fearing
Your daughter's brain is disappearing.

There's nothing left of KayCee's self,
So take her home and find a shelf
Where she can lie, warm, dry and clean
To be an answering machine."

Suzy

I'm not sure Mr Belloc would have approved of this one. The grisly fate is not actually suffered by the one the caution is aimed at. Read on…

The moment Suzy Plumley-Wilde
Discovered she might be with child,
She started on a new regime
And hired experts -- what a team!
An obstetrician (Harley Street),
Chiropodist to mind her feet,
Psychiatrist, a fan of Freud,
A trainer who would be employed
In making sure that Mrs P.
Was fit for childbirth, something he
Most diligently undertook,
And lastly one who wrote the book
On giving babies just what's best:
"Not formula, you fool, but breast!"

Now, aided by her husband, who
Once led a trek to Timbuktu,
Our preggers lady organised
A list so long you'd be surprised
Of things that parents ought to know
Of infants when in utero.
To give the budding brain a boost,
Try playing Mozart, reading Proust
In French *and* English, so the tot
May well emerge a polyglot.
To calm the agitated whelp
meditation's such a help.
No drink, no drugs, no cigarettes,
No flying supersonic jets
(A thing that she was wont to do
Before this baby thing came through)

But now the forty weeks are done,
The oven spawns this well-cooked bun.
Let's skip the actual birthing part;
We know they scream, we know they fart.
We know they..... Draw the curtain here;
Some things are far too gross I fear.
Fast forward for a week or so
As baby Fleur begins to grow...
According to the latest creed,
Now Suzy's teaching her to read.
At one she's learning how to speak -
At first in Latin, then in Greek.
In Mandarin, Italian, French;
Ah, what a clever little wench!
At two, with very little fuss,
She's mastered all of calculus.
By three she has some expertise
In astrophysics, if you please.

And so it goes, her Mum's ambition
Forever leads to more tuition.
Philosophy and Russian Lit.
It seems that Suzy just won't quit.
She's stuffing in her daughter's brain,
More subjects than the King of Spain.
You think that's all? Oh no, not yet;
There's violin and clarinet,
There's opera, blues and swing and rap,
There's ballet, hip-hop, jazz and tap...

Where is this going? Can you tell?
The poor girl's head began to swell.
With information overloaded,
Her brain quite suddenly exploded,
Making such a dreadful mess
On Cousin Margot's brand new dress,
And splattering some awful goo
On Grandma, who at ninety-two,

Had seen such horrors in the Blitz
As half her family blown to bits,
And now remarked, *"Please have the grace
To detonate some other place."*

Now Fleur has gone to life eternal
And Suzy's left with thoughts maternal:
*"I never meant her head to burst;
Next time I'll teach survival first!"*

Zachary

This one adds a touch of political satire. Up to you to choose which leader Zachary most resembles.

Young Zachary lacked any smidgen of tact;
He would often say *"Boo!"* to his mother.
Then to his papa, he'd *"Ahoy!"* and *"Aha!";*
He would do much the same to his brother.

When he ran through the town with his smile upside down,
The passers-by shied in confusion
At the size of his eyes and his constant loud cries.
He swore and profaned in profusion.

"Alack and alas! I will not go to Mass!"
He shouted till Shoreham was shaken.
*"If you think I'll be scammed and my poor noggin crammed
With nonsense like that, you're mistaken."*

As he passed by the zoo, he'd go *"Hi!"* and *"Halloo!"*
"Avast ye!" and *"High cockalorum!"*
Till the hyenas howled and the mad monkeys yowled,
Like any political forum.

At school he would cough, till the teacher cried *"Off
To the Principal's office, you vermin!"*
But as Zack left the room, he'd cry *"Fie! Va va voom!"*
Just why, no one there could determine.

Then as the lad grew he would spout out anew
These expostulations atrocious:
"Caramba! Cor Blimey! Oy Vey, Little Hymie!"
And *"Super XP Alidocious!"*

Through Eton he blundered, while all the world wondered
Just how they'd survive the upheaval.
"You villainous varlet! You hasty-wit harlot!"
Snarled Zachary, all medieval.

At Oxford he screamed at the spires as they dreamed;
The dons neither scared him nor scarred him.
"Tally-ho! Chocks away!" he was oft heard to say,
And the Tories soon marked him for stardom.

"You skivers, you skanks!" saw him rise through the ranks;
"Sieg Heil!" revealed motives more sinister.
"You plebs to your prison! Your Prince has arisen!"
In a trice he was voted Prime Minister.

While stock-markets jittered, Zack tweeted and twittered
At any who dared to rebuke him.
"Well, Alla Kazam! Good Golly! Godamn!
There's no option left but to nuke 'em."

Oh, the missiles that flew and the tantrums he threw;
"Malarkey! Baloney! Gazinter!"
In a week at the most, the globe gave up the ghost
And collapsed into nuclear winter.

Then Zack (who'd survived) knew he'd really arrived
And sought out some cronies to cheer him.
"I hurrah! Zippy Dee!" he chortled with glee...

.. but no one was left who could hear him.

Tommy,
who wouldn't brush his teeth

We do all brush – and floss – don't we?!

Little Tommy Tiddly-Pom would never brush his teeth
So they turned all black and yellow, but with green stuff underneath.
He'd never need a costume when it came to Halloween -
Just open wide, say, *"Look inside -- it's yellow, black and green."*

When little Tommy went to school, the kids all screamed and cried;
They jeered and joked and pushed and poked and ran away to hide.
When Tommy-Pom turned ten his mouth had green stuff growing out,
Like silver beet and broccoli and icky brussels sprout.

The dentist came to see and said, *"Alas, 'tis as I feared -
Your gums have got so gunky that your teeth have disappeared.
I think I see a pine tree and a grove of eucalyptus;
They told such tales in dental school -- by golly, how they gripped us!"*

*"There's only one thing for it; could you fetch the chainsaw, Nurse?
Then bring an axe, we have to act, before things get much worse."*
They tied young Tommy to a chair; the chainsaw roared and growled;
The axe was swung with vigour, while the frightened patient howled.

And when the trees had fallen, in the undergrowth beneath
They found the scattered remnants of poor Tommy's tortured teeth.
Though Tommy's future's cloudy, there's a silver lining here -
They had green vegies for a month and firewood for a year!

Bullivant Bradley

The whole point of a Cautionary Tale is that the perpetrator gets to meet a grisly fate. Is Bullivant's lot better or worse than most?

There once was a boy, name of Bullivant Bradley,
Who topped the whole world in behaving most badly.
He'd spend the whole morning in snarling and sneering;
When the afternoon came he'd be taunting and jeering.

His classmates, his teacher, his principal too,
All asked him to stop it, but inside they knew
That Bullivant wouldn't *or couldn't* behave -
The more that you begged the more trouble he gave.

He teased all the dogs and he pulled the cats' tails,
Tormented the girls and then laughed at their wails;
And Bullivant then started in on the boys;
He called them bad names and he broke their best toys.

Now poor Mrs Pring from the green-grocer's shop
Was taken quite poorly when out he did pop
From behind the bananas, with beans in his ears.
(They say she'll be better in one or two years!)

And Paul the policeman, a mild-mannered fellow,
Forgot all his manners and let out a bellow
When Bullivant Bradley, dressed up as a clown,
Dived into the pool and pretended to drown.

Now, children, I'll tell you a boy who's a beast
May still grow to be a most venerable priest,
A fireman, a soldier, a doctor, a plumber,
A lifeguard patrolling the beach in the summer,

But surely a thug like young Bullivant Bradley
Is bound to go wrong and to end up quite sadly?
But that's where you're wrong, nothing sordid or sinister:
He went into politics - now he's Prime Minister!

Haydon, who ran with scissors

Perhaps you have heard of the Darwin Awards which salute the improvement of the human genome by honouring those who accidentally remove themselves from it in a spectacular manner! Young Haydon would make a fine nominee.

There's one thing you should always tell
Your children, till they've learnt it well;
Don't run with scissors; sure disaster
Awaits the child who will not master
Maxims thus so sagely stated.

Now I think that you have waited
Long enough; let's meet the boy,
His mother's pride, his father's joy,
Haydon Reginald McMurray,
Who never walked when he could scurry.

He was a lovely lad it seemed,
He threw no tantrums, seldom screamed,
He ate his carrots, spinach too,
And even kissed his Aunty Sue
(Despite the thick moustache she grew.)

This paragon, this sweet confection,
Had just the *tiniest* imperfection:
Though oftentimes he had been told,
Berated, chided, coaxed, cajoled,
He would not slow his impetus
When holding sharpish blades. A fuss
Is what they're making, so he thought.
Alas, he just could not be taught!

One day, with scissors in his hand
This little chap was running, and
Tripped on the cat. The fur went flying
As Haydon lay there loudly crying.

Oh, what a rumpus! What a ruction!
The organs used for reproduction
Were severed quite, beyond repairing.
Then how his parents grew despairing.

They cried, *"Oh, no! Oh, what a shame!*
However shall our fam'ly name
Be blessed, continued and extended?
The proud McMurray line has ended."

Let's close the page on Haydon's yelling.
The moral's clear; you don't need telling;
Don't run with scissors, it's just silly -
You may do damage to your willy!

Bathroom Incident

Sadly, this tale is based on personal experience. Fortunately, it doesn't qualify me for the Darwin Awards.

O, gentle reader, if ye be male,
Beware! The ending to this tale
May cause a shock, a tic, a judder,
Or worse, involuntary shudder.

On the other hand, the fairer sex,
(Those with chromosome double X),
May on the floor with laughter die
With teardrops streaming from each eye.

My yarn begins in harmless style;
I had not showered for a while.
Sweat and dirt and caked on grime
And pungent odour proclaimed, "It's time!"

So off to the bathroom I did trot,
Turned on the taps, both cold and hot.
The streaming jets at once did spurt,
As I removed my pants and shirt.

In the maelstrom I'd created
My weary body luxuriated.
I shampooed, soaped and shower-gelled too
Till slather-lather bubbles flew.

An age I plied the cleansing art
And scrubbed and rinsed each body part
Till flushed and pink like a beauty queen,
I could proclaim, *"I'm clean, I'm clean!"*

The taps are turned, the torrent stilled,
Leaving just a pool where it was spilled.
A towel's at hand; before I grab it,
There's one more act, by force of habit.

From my body so clean and slick
The excess water I must flick.
First my tummy and then my back
And then each arm I did attack.

There's one part left as you will see,
The back of legs from arse to knee.
Now I'm not one to chatter, me,
But now we need some anatomy.

Do you recall the birds and bees-
The male and female properties?
And how, between the legs there lies,
A sensitive package unique to guys?

The penile shaft, that masculine totem
And the tactile sac they label 'scrotum'?
All nerve endings are centred here
With guilt and pleasure and pain and fear.

Some say, "*Size, it doesn't count.
Well maybe just the least amount.*"
But I'll admit to being proud
To be one of the truly well-endowed.

"*Vive la différence!*" they say,
But that's what caused the tears that day,
For flying fingers floorwards flashing,
Struck that sac, and my world came crashing.

Oh what a truly grievous error,
Before the pain, a sense of terror;
Then agony struck like a lightning bolt,
A fierce, intense, electric jolt.

Blood-curdling is too weak a word
To describe the shriek that then was heard.
Down the leafy suburban street,
Dogs leaped startled to their feet.

Neighbours to their doors did rush
To spy what shattered the Sunday hush,
Terrified birds flew from their nests,
Mothers clutched infants to their breasts.

Windows shattered, alarm bells clanged,
Old deaf folk muttered, *"I'll be danged!"*
Through city blocks it penetrated,
Round ragged rooftops reverberated.

On bathroom tiles, I still was lying,
Whining, whinging, whimpering, crying.
My darling, 'She who must be obeyed',
Investigated the racket made,

Surveyed my pitiful cringing plight,
And tenderly asked, *"Are you alright?"*
I told my tale and shortly after
More screams were heard, this time of laughter.

It seems no sympathy avails
To one who's so far off the rails
For breaking one of life's golden rules:
'You must always protect the family jewels.'

People Who Live in Grass Houses...

Most proverbs are Cautionary Tales by another name. This poem is based on such a proverb and I'll admit to borrowing the plot from that wonderful old BBC radio programme "My Word" which challenged the linguistically inventive team of Frank Muir and Denis Norden to ad lib a twisted version of well-known phrases.

On the island of KitchyKaiYu
Lived a king and a queen (Yes, it's true!)
They rested their bones
On a pair of stone thrones
On cushions of course (wouldn't you?)

One day (it may well have been summer)
As they sat with their butts growing number
Through endless orations
By tribal legations
The pair grew both grimmer and glummer.

In their palace of grass (old colonial)
They sat on those seats ceremonial
Till the queen's derriere
Was so reddened and rare
That she threatened the peace matrimonial.

That night as they massaged their sorrow
The queen cried, *"Let's beg, steal or borrow.
I've a catalogue here
From Roebuck and Sear.
I'm ordering new chairs tomorrow!"*

'Twas done. Soon the royal posterior
Was seated on softness superior.
The queen was emphatic,
*"Those old thrones to the attic!
They're clogging the palace interior."*

Now the ending is far from appealing
(Turn away if you're tender of feeling)
For the weight quite inordinate
Of stone thrones they'd stored in it
Proved more than a match for the ceiling.

The fate of the royals lamentable
Shows even the monarchy's dentable
Their Highnesses splatter
Like pancakes (but flatter)
The enquiry said *"This was preventable."*

The couple's untimely demise
Has a moral not hard to surmise:
If your home's made of grass
Don't be such an ass
To stow thrones; it's prob'ly not wise!

ROUND THE BLOCK

Around ten years ago, She Who Must be Obeyed (henceforth referred to as SWMBO) and I returned from a 12-year stint raising the average IQ of Australia, to live in Northland, New Zealand. The dilapidated house, bought sight unseen on TradeMe, and the tiny patch of land were our version of a lifestyle block. Hence the title of this section. The next 13 poems are all inspired in one way or another by living the dream à la Tom and Barbara in The Good Life.

The Great Escaper Caper

We have a paddock – too steep to be easily mowed. The obvious answer is goats. As we soon found, goats are delightful but come with their own issues. With a slight nod to a variety of WWII POW escape stories, read on!

They're a pair of horned Houdinis,
You might even call them genies
And their appetite for mischief is immense.
One is Maya, one is Lucy
They believe that grass is juicy
When it's growing on the far side of the fence.

I'm the one who did the digging,
Built the fence with all its rigging,
More secure than Colditz Castle, so I thought.
They went under, over, round it;
Where a loophole lay they found it
And went munching on the things they didn't ought.
Like a magnet to their noses
Were the most expensive roses,
While the flower border never stood a chance.
Through the spinach, beets and rocket,
Adding health foods to their docket,
They continued on their free and merry dance.

Now the umpteenth sortie's ended
And once more the fence is mended,
There'll be peace now for a little while at least.
See them round the pen go trotting,
Now with beards together, plotting;
They are cooking up another breakout feast.

But this time I'll have them beaten;
Not another shrub gets eaten,
Not another Queen Elizabeth destroyed,
For I've called up my supplier,
Bought more coils of razor wire;
The perimeter has landmines all deployed.

There are searchlights that will function
Set at every gate and junction,
With motion sensors, cameras and the like.
See their yellow eyes a-gleaming;
I won't fear their sneaky scheming -
Each plan defeated by pre-emptive strike.

Now I just can't help but wonder
If I made a silly blunder,
When I gave that goatish pair a vaulting horse;
And it's rather hard to follow
Why the ground here rings so hollow
And their bleating sounds like little bursts of Morse.

What's that Maya's got beside 'er?
Could it be a working glider?
And where did Lucy get that set of keys?
Raise the shields round all the flowers!
Snipers, quickly mount your towers -
And someone send for reinforcements, PLEASE....

Palais de Poop

First goats, then chickens. Whatever were we thinking?

Lily and Milly and Chocolate and Alice,
The resident birds down at Cluckingham Palace
All scurried away as I hove into view
With my shovel and rake and my wheelbarrow too.

See, chickens are lovely, they're cute and they're gentle,
They never take time off, parental or dental,
But they do have a habit which gets to a chap -
They're prone to producing vast mountains of crap.

Oh, yes, it's that day when I clean out the coop,
The Gulag of Guano, the Palais de Poop.
I'll be shovelling shit in the Dungeon of Dung,
More smelly and black than a coal-miner's lung.

So here I am wading through muck to my knees
While stooped at an angle of ninety degrees.
My nose is assaulted by pungent aroma -
I'm cramped, cracked and crazy and close to a coma.

One thought still sustains me, one concept revives:
My struggle brings succour to so many lives.
My beans all say thank you, my rhubarb salutes
As chooky-poo manna refreshes their roots.

Chillis, tomatoes and aubergines too
All thrive on this wonderful, life-giving goo.
A green thumb will tell you there's never a match
For chicken manure on your vegetable patch.

The Coat-Tail Ghost

This entertaining tale and the one that follows, The Great Weta Catastrophe, both have their roots in my childhood years growing up in rural NZ. My father used to tell this story and swore it was true. All I have done is put it into verse and given a little poetic licence to some of the details.

Come, gather round, all o' you young'uns
While I rest me weary bones.
Come closer to the campfire
And turn off them mobile phones!

There's a tale I'd like to tell ya
Cos, it won't mean much to most,
About the night that I encountered
A coat-tail tugging ghost.

Back then our phones stayed on the wall,
We had no TV set,
No danglin' iPod gizmos,
Nor no flamin' internet.

Now, Fred, that's not the scary part,
No need to look so tearful.
A life without your Facebook friends
Ain't really sumpin' fearful.

Now, me and Len and Tom were mates
Like those famous Moose-keteers.
'Twas all for one and one for all
Through sunshine, rain and tears.

This day, we're sittin' feelin bored
Wi' nowt much else to do,
When Tommy spins this frightful yarn
About the ghost of Dan Carew.

See, folks round there said Dan trapped kids
And ground their bones for dinner.
He was a strange one, that's for sure,
A proper Loony Binner.

Though he was dead and buried
In that ol' graveyard on the hill,
Some people claimed his spirit roamed
And preyed on children still.

Oh, I was young and foolish then
And prone to silly boasts;
My trap I opened up and cried,
"I'm not afraid of ghosts!"

Then Len and Tom, my two best friends
They hatched a cunning plot
To make me eat my reckless words
And put me on the spot.

They dared me to confront the ghost
At midnight in the church.
A shiver of dread ran down my spine
And my heart gave a kind of lurch.

But to Tommy and Len I spoke boldly,
Not showing a quiver of fear.
"I'll do it," I vowed. "At eleven tonight
Make sure that you meet me here."

Well, late that night as a storm brewed up,
Sane folk in their safe beds slept,
While we three scamps through our windows slipped
And down the dark road crept.

Then an eerie, moaning wind sprang up
And the rain came helter-skelter,
As we paused for a bit at the graveyard fence
Where the lych-gate gave us shelter.

Our torch-lights played o'er the drunken stones
Where the dead lay eternally sleeping,
And the rain tumbled down in torrents
As if God himself was a-weeping.

"It's time," whispered Tom, and he thrust in my hand
A hammer and a six-inch nail.
"At the altar's foot you must mark the spot,
So we know that you did not fail."

With a slap on my back and a cheery *"Good luck,"*
The two settled down to wait,
While I plunged into the gloomy dark
To meet with my ghostly fate.

You kids wouldn't know about terror,
How it melts all your bones to a mush;
The tremblin' hands and the chatterin' teeth,
Stark fear that comes in a rush.

But I tell you, that night I felt terror,
As sure as I'm talkin' to you,
For I knew in the dark church lay waiting
The ghost of the mad Dan Carew.

For a moment I thought he had found me
And I gave out a sort of a howl.
With a whoosh and a flash it flew past me-
'Twas just a harmless old owl.

The old door creaked noisily open,
I came back to my senses again;
I took a few steps t'ward the altar.
At least I was out of that rain.

Then I knelt at the front, by the prayer rail
Where thousands had pleaded their plight,
But I doubt that their prayers were as urgent
As the one that I muttered that night.

The torch I laid down as I hammered
Cast shadows of fear round the room
And I knew as I stood to start fleeing
That I'd hammered the way to my doom.

For a great ghostly hand from the darkness
Gave my coat-tails a bit of a tweak.
Though I struggled and fought, he held tighter,
Till I let out an almighty shriek.

I could smell Dan Carew at my shoulder,
I could feel his foul breath at my throat,
And I couldn't abide to be eaten
So I tore loose his grip on my coat.

Home I streaked, my raincoat in tatters,
With Lenny and Tom at my heels,
And I told how the ghost had clung to me,
How he'd planned I'd be one of his meals.

In the cold light of day we went back there,
Just Lenny and Tommy and me.
We checked out the nail that I'd driven,
And the answer was quite plain to see.

Now the God-fearin' folk of that county,
Will still give a bit of a roar,
When they tell of the young fool at midnight
Who nailed his own coat to the floor.

The Great Weta Catastrophe

Another story with more than a grain of truth in its inception.
Enjoy!

Times were hard and getting harder in our sleepy little town;
Luck had hit a rocky bottom - then had kept on drillin' down.
An' them that had an ounce of sense had packed their bags and fled,
But we, poor fools, like Murphy's mules, had stuck it out instead.

Us kids, we all wore hand-me-downs since Ginty's Mill had closed;
There were patches on our patches - that was normal, we supposed.
We had meat to eat on Sundays, but don't ask me what it were-
Tho' Monday's soup was greyish gloop of boiled-up bones and fur.

One day, way down by Big Bing's Bush, I met this strange galoot,
With spotless, shining city shoes and a fancy city suit.
"I say, young man," this geezer purred, *"may I seek your assistance?*
I'm in the lurch when on the search for wetas - each one's sixpence."

Dear readers, please forgive me if I spend a while digressin'
For it could be that you missed, one day, that Nature Studies lesson.
A bug that's most misunderstood, the common garden weta,
Is seldom met by those who get a latte with their feta.

If you're creepy-crawly-phobic, then I guess you'd run a mile,
Cos there's somethin' quite alarmin' 'bout a weta's friendly smile.
See, he's big and brown and scaly like a cancerous carbuncle-
All spines and legs, Ma Nature's dregs, a roach's nightmare uncle.

But he's really rather lovely, he won't nip you if you're gentle,
Just don't drop one down Suzy's front, she's liable to go mental!
He's not noted for destruction or malicious interference;
Like snail and slug, this ugly bug's maligned for his appearance.

Turns out this city-slicker sort was somethin' scientific
Who thought inspectin' insects was a pastime quite terrific.
I shook his hand, I sealed the deal, inside my brain was buzzin'-
Me arithmetic I'd worked out quick - six shillings for a dozen.

My head it whirled with dreams of wealth, I'd be my fam'ly's saviour;
I'd be lauded and applauded for exemplary behaviour.
Before his back was turned I'd found the first of my collection
Without a thought that what I caught was headin' for dissection.

Through gulleys full of tea-tree, up hill, down dale, I plodded.
I peered and prised and poked and pried; each totara stump I
prodded.
One dozen wetas in one hour, one dozen hours per day;
I'd plant my feet on Easy Street when I got my first week's pay.

Still my head was full of numbers, they was whizzin' round and
round-
Twelve hundred wetas, more or less - t'was close to thirty pound!
We'd eat roast beef three times a week, there'd be new clothes for all-
Can't be denied, that kind of pride is headin' for a fall.

I'd made a weta prison out of plywood from the shed
And I kept those critters captive in a box beneath my bed.
There'd be pleasure for the buyer and a treasure for the seller-
Next day the Prof would cart them off and I'd be Rockefeller.

Was it carelessness at lock-up time or just a twist of fate?
At dawn a thousand wetas simply burst out from their crate.
Angry, hungry, out they marched, a well-drilled insect army;
By instinct urged, onwards they surged, a terrible tsunami.

Six thousand feet a-scuttlin' swiftly jolted me awake
As a tragedy unfolded and my heart began to break;

There were thirty in the pantry, there were fifty in the sink,
A hundred more hopped out the door before I'd time to think.

The dog slunk frightened from his bed with weird, unearthly wail,
A weta tangled in each ear and five more on his tail.
My sister Suzy started screaming, waking brother Davy
Who thundered out and mashed about creating weta gravy

Now Dad was in the 'Reading Room' - what we called his long
retreat-
When six big wetas scrambled out from underneath the seat.
Well, his screamin' woke the echoes and they fiercely answered back-
A wily one had sought to run, for refuge, up a crack.

There are wetas that are runners, there are wetas that are stickers;
Seems several of the latter sort had stuck on Mother's knickers.
Now, I love my parents dearly, they're not prone to acts aggressive,
But what came next left me perplexed and bordered on obsessive,

For my mother took a frying pan, my father took a spade;
They whomped on ev'ry weta there that wriggled, breathed or prayed.
Now my buttocks still are stingin' and my backside's fiery red;
When they couldn't get a weta then they whaled on me instead.

In the midst of all the ruckus, as I shuddered, weak and shivery,
My friendly vivisectionist rolled up to take delivery.
There was not a living weta to be found for miles around'
My toil and pain had been in vain - farewell my thirty pound!

There I stood amongst the carnage and my lip began to twitch;
As I mourned my friends the wetas who'd been goin' to
make me rich.
Oh, they say a loving family's the only thing that matters,
But it's tragic when the magic of a dream is torn to tatters

Murder in the Cowshed

Our 'block' borders a dairy farm, so we get the pleasure of watching the cows wend their way up to the shed to be milked, while avoiding what I learned in my rural upbringing was the tedious chore of actually milking them. Those childhood memories stirred my imagination to pen this murder with no mystery. If it seems vaguely familiar, it has been published before in the Lifestyle Block magazine.

Funny how death sneaks up on you
And gives you a kind of a grab;
One day you may sing of the pleasures of spring;
The next you're ice-cold on a slab.

Take Zachary Johnson for instance,
A young man of infinite charm,
Good looking and clever, all rural endeavour,
Milking two hundred cows on the farm.

Now Zach was an old-fashioned fella'
As gentle and sweet as they came.
Every cow in the herd received a kind word
As he greeted each one by her name.

So Maisie and Bella and Katie
Would all feel the warmth of his hands.
To his touch soft as silk they would let down their milk
As he massaged their mammary glands.

But even a farmer has favourites
And in this Zach was just like the rest.
Lying close to his heart, two heifers so smart,
Were the ones he considered his best.

All black and white splotches was Jessie,
A monochromatic delight,
From her dainty white feet to her face, oh so sweet,
A Friesian to love at first sight.

And equally lovely was Bessie,
A Jersey both gentle and wise.
Her coat shining gold was a joy to behold;
You could drown in her liquid brown eyes.

All creatures need love and attention;
It's a key to their very survival.
A storm began brewing while Jessie stood chewing;
She perceived Bessie now as a rival.

Now bovine psychology's tricky,
For that any farmer can vouch.
Sigmund Freud in his prime couldn't foresee the crime
For you can't fit a cow on a couch.

See, a cow is a ruminant creature,
Looking peaceful behind that farm gate,
But as Jessie chewed cud, bitter jealousy's bud
Blossomed into a great flower of hate.

The motive was clear, the means lay at hand,
Opportunity not far beyond,
And Zach, with a crash and a soggy kersplash,
Flew into the effluent pond.

Now your average cow on an average day
Emits a small mountain of waste.
And then multiply, that's a mighty big pie
Of mucky and yucky green paste.

A week's worth would swallow a mammoth,
In a month you could launch a small ship,
And I'd have to say, with a fragrant bouquet
That it's far from ideal for a dip.

Sad to say that young Zach was no swimmer
And his gumboots they weighted him down.
Four hundred sad eyes all saw his demise
As the herd watched poor Zachary drown.

Now Marple and Maigret and Holmes and Poirot,
Columbo and Lord Peter Wimsey
Would have to concede that this case has them treed,
The evidence faint, flawed and flimsy.

Two hundred witnesses, all of them mute,
(Apart from the odd burp or moo),
No noose gun or knife that may take a man's life.
No body – that's still in the poo.

Though Bessie the Jersey may roll her brown eyes,
Fair Jessie walks free as a bird.
The old farmer's sunk but the new one's a hunk
"And my God, those warm hands! Have you heard?"

I'll See You Dead

For those who care about such trivial matters, this form of poetry with a repeated motif line is called a Rondeau. Otherwise, just make sure you catch the punchline with its wry comment about one of the downsides of life in the country.

"I'll see you dead!" my love declared.
"Your time is up! You'll not be spared!
Just mark my words - this day you'll rue.
if I can lay my hands on you."
... and in my study, I sat scared.

Out there, her anger fumed and flared;
her lips were curled, her teeth were bared.
She cried until the spittle flew,
"I'll see you dead!"

Against such fury, unprepared,
I would have run, if I had dared.
A silent terror, then I knew.
She swore until the air turned blue,
to ev'ry fly she flayed or snared,
"I'll see you dead!"

Thank God I'm Unemployed

Some of these 'Round the Block' tales run to high levels of hyperbole and even (Gasp!) fiction. The more I re-read this one, the more I see how close to reality it is!

Them goats are full of hi jinks,
They're up to their old tricks;
They've gone and bust the fence again -
It needs another fix.

The sweet corn's lookin' nibbled
Bin a possum there no doubt.
We'll have to get it picked today;
No way to keep him out.

The lawns they all need mowin'
Though they're straggly parched and brown,
And SWMBO[1] says food stocks are low;
We'd best shoot into town.

The old shed's been dismantled
Just to make a chicken coop.
The bits are strewn along the fence -
Them chooks are in the soup!

The tank's run dry, I rang the guy
To see how much per tanker.
Four hundred bucks! He must be mad!
He's just a bloody ...... banker!

Those cats that both adopted us
Are yet to see the vet.
But the bathroom's nearly finished...
Well nearly .... not quite.... yet.

There's beans, tomatoes, cucumbers,
A-pilin' on the table;
We'll get them frozen and preserved
Just as soon as we are able.

And that reminds me, how the heck
Are veggies meant to grow,
When there ain't no blimmin' water?
That's what I'd like to know.

The house is half-way painted;
I'll get it done, no fear.
It's only bin six months so far...
Perhaps another year.

I'll fix the windows, spray the weeds,
Unblock the kitchen sink,
Trim the goats' hooves, bathe the dogs,
So they no longer stink.

Spring clean the house. Aunt Mavis may
Come visitin' next week;
The car is due a warrant
And the steerin' needs a tweak.

We'd better spray those fruit trees there;
Their leaves are turnin' black.
The neighbour's cow's out on the road;
Let's go and drive her back,

Then chop and stack the firewood
And fix that leaky tap;
The water pump's gone on the fritz,
The front gate has a gap,

Prune the roses, dig the spuds,
Repair the back steps too
Make sure the dogs have water,
Then scrape up the chicken poo.

When I survey my list of chores
It makes me kinda dizzy.
Thank God I'm flamin' unemployed
Or I'd be really busy!

1. Remember Rumpole of the Bailey, that curiously lovable character created by writer John Mortimer and then developed into legendary status by the acting genius of Leo McKern in the long-running TV series? Rumpole always referred to his wife as 'She Who Must Be Obeyed' or SWMBO. I have lovingly adopted this monicker for my own wife and she appears thus in several of my poems. In this case, it should be pronounced as Swim-Bo

Me and Spiggo-Thingo

True tale, with just a tiny bit of exaggeration in the details. My doctor is a lovely man and I'd like to share this poem with him, but I'm just too worried about how he might receive the description of his waiting room!

A free health check, that's what it said, that letter in the post;
Now, I'm a bloke who does enjoy a freebie more than most.
The missus seemed to think it wise, I'm sure she wasn't nagging,
Just gently stating point of view with frequent finger-wagging.

If there's one thing I've learnt in life, unless the body's failing,
It's wise to keep away from people likely to be ailing.
You may say I'm an optimist, you may say I'm a cynic,
I had to get, from my sweet pet, directions to the clinic.

I'm sure that doctors' rooms are scrubbed, they're pristine and they're gleaming,
But then they fill them up with folk whose orifices streaming
Show measles, mumps and whooping cough; they've fever, flu and ague
With scurvy, boils and pestilence and other ills that plague you.

There's petulance and flatulence and verbal diarrhoea;
There's ADD and STD. TB and gonorrhoea.
Into this sneezing, wheezing horde, with fear and trepidation,
I ventured timidly and sat amongst the congregation.

I took a seat with terror for I mingled with bacteria;
There on my left sat chicken pox and on my right diphtheria;
Across the room lurked cholera, behind me lay malaria,
Oh what relief, my stay was brief within this lethal area.

At first the nurse was nice as pie; she smiled, she laughed, she joked,
And all the while with expert eye she prodded, pried and poked.
My weight, my height, my heart, my sight, my family history too;
Each box was checked to sweet effect, she said, *"We're almost through."*

And then she pulled this gadget out, a thing of steely glitter;
She bound one end around my arm and then fired up the critter.
While Spiggo-nano-saurus gave my arm a thorough mauling,
The nurse sat listening to the news, it must have been enthralling.

You could tell the thing was broken by the way she paused and frowned,
Then shook her head and tapped the glass and twirled it round and round.
"Let's try that one more time," she said and pressed the starting trigger;
The monster grabbed my arm again with 'strordinary vigour.

Once more she listened with intent and what she heard, it shocked 'er.
"Wait here," she said. *"Don't move an inch, I'll run and fetch the doctor"*
The good man came with soothing words to ease my apprehension,
"Old chap, I'd say that what you've got's a spot of hypertension."

*"Our Spiggo-thingo reckons that you've cracked a double-ton.
If all our batsmen scored like you, we'd show those Aussies fun!
I have some pills will cure your ills; just take one every day.
I guarantee that your BP will soon be A-OK!"*

"Look here," I cried, *"I came today, a happy, healthy man;
I sat there in your Hall of Horrors; p'raps that was your plan.
Out there's a bloke whose gut's as big as Mikey's Monster Marrow.
I don't know how he fetched it here unless he used a barrow."*

And over in the corner, that old dear so still and gray -
She's far from well and by the smell, she's maybe passed away.
I've risked my life just coming here midst bugs of all descriptions;
The pall of doom within that room has given me conniptions.

I'm off back home to take a bath in water disinfected
To kill the germs and bugs and worms that I have here collected.
I'll take your pill, I swear I will, and thanks for your assistance,
But from henceforth both south and north, I'm going to keep my distance!"

Mad Poets' Society

We all love to complain about the weather. This poem and the one that follows highlight the 'flood or drought' mantra that farmers often recite. On that topic, I advise you to go google the poem 'Said Hanrahan' by Australian bush poet John O'Brien. How a few of my favourite poets got caught up in this piece of silliness is simply a product of my warped imagination.

The rain is coming down in sheets;
"It's wet me bum!" Walt Whitman bleats.
And thus, say Wordsworth, Byron, Keats,
"It won't stop bloody raining!"

A river's flowing down the path;
"Let's step outside and take a bath,"
McGough tells Hughes, who then tells Plath,
"It won't stop bloody raining!"

Outside, a lake is rippling,
(Though Hopkins would say 'stippling')
while Tennyson and Kipling
cry, **"It won't stop bloody raining!"**

Now Shakespeare takes a swim; he's lost,
where all the waves are tempest-tossed,
and this from Shelley, Donne and Frost:
"It won't stop bloody raining!"

The house is floating -- off we go.
"We're catching up with Willy, though,"
call Yeats and Dickinson and Poe.
"It won't stop bloody raining!"

So down the stream, across the lake,
till Walter Scott yells, **_"Where's the brake?"_**
To Carroll, Coleridge and Blake,
"It won't stop bloody raining!"

At last our good ship runs aground,
and listen, what's that pleasing sound?
It's Hardy, Angelou and Pound -
"Thank God it's not still raining!"

It's Dry Again

Yeah, just go back and read the intro to the previous piece!

It's dry again, the earth has cracks
would swallow Grandma in her tracks,
if she should wander off the path.
Don't flush the loo! Don't take a bath!
We're saving every precious drop
to nourish our remaining crop,
a solitary runner bean;
it's all we have; and food trumps clean.

It's dry again, so if you must
walk on the road, beware the dust.
It swallowed grandpa yesterday -
(an extra bean for me - Hooray!)
I saw a cloud just now, I did,
but then it bloody went and hid
behind a wall of solid blue;
the sun beats down on me and you.

It's dry again, the water tank
holds only echoes. At the bank,
they've called our mortgage in. Oh dear!
They'll have to stand in line, I fear;
we haven't got a single bean -
oh, that's not true, but what I mean -
we do not have a brass razoo,
a dime, a cent or any clue
how we can make a cup of tea
except from our recycled wee...
It's dry again...

Note to Self

Sadly, one of a few poems here that are based on fact! Also the shortest poem in this book. Important, advice, though. Perhaps it would be better placed in the Cautionary Tales!

Note to self:
When you've chopped chilli,
Keep your hands off
Your damn willy!

The Machine Stops

They say things happen in threes. When it comes to household appliances, it seems to me that they happen in dozens! The title is a reference to a great Sci-Fi short story by E. M. Forster.

The fridge is far from frosty
and the toaster's on the fritz;
the mower's scattered round the yard
in countless shattered bits.

The kettle gives a deathly wail
then, whimpering, expires;
the stereo's demented
Like a dozen off-key choirs.

The washer's bumpy-thumping
like it wants to leave the room;
the heater's grown quite chilly
and the oven's met its doom.

The waste disposal ate four forks
then graunched before exploding;
there's a message on the microwave
that fills me with foreboding.

The telly's just gone belly-up
smack in the evening news;
the DVD needs TLC;
computer's blown a fuse.

My Bluetooth needs a dentist
and my Wi-Fi's disconnected;
my razor flicked its flexy tail
then died; how unexpected!

My iPad tells me I don't know
the year that I was born;
my smart phone's lost its smarts it seems;
my Kindle's reading porn.

My GPS has lost its way
and beggared off to Burma;
my Whipper-Snipper slipped and dipped,
then ate some terra firma

I'd like to post this poem on-line
so all the world can read it,
but the Internet's gone Poof! Kaput!
just when I really need it!

The Other Side

I swear the first two lines are true – well apart from the Utakura
River being described as swift and foaming. After that my
imagination took over!

When I was young, I lived across
a river swift and foaming.
Alas, three siblings had I lost,
who went a-reckless roaming.
There was a bridge, a kind of plank;
the brave would sometimes risk it,
but many fell and many sank
before they'd eat our biscuit.

My one remaining sister, Flo,
cried out, *"Who shall I marry?*
That bloody river swallowed Joe -
and Tom and Dick and Harry!
I fancied Robert; in he went,
and Albert followed after.
Then Phil and George, on courting bent,
but now they'll never hafter."

Me mother too was feeling blue -
supplies were hard to gather.
The butcher and the grocer too
were frightened to a lather.
They'd sometimes hurl a bag across
with mutton or a carrot,
but mostly we just dined on moss
like poets in a garret.

A starving wretch, one day I planned
to brave the brimming river.

I'd rather die, you understand,
than sigh and starve and shiver.
A boat's the thing to ease our plight,
a jolly little schooner.
I'll have it built this very night.
'Twere wise I'd done it sooner.

And so 'twas done, I made the thing,
a pretty barque and sturdy.
And as I worked, began to sing,
as sweet as any birdie.
"The Conqueror" I named my boat
and painted that upon it.
To Ma and Pa I proudly wrote
a bonny farewell sonnet.

The time was nigh, the river high
in torrents swiftly streaming.
I launched my craft and cried goodbye -
of freedom I was dreaming.
Just like a feather in the breeze,
my ship went freely whirling
amidst the tumult of the seas,
above me great waves curling.

I cursed myself, I cried aloud,
'Twas just as I was fearing.
My grand design - I'd been so proud -
had got no means of steering.
Ahead I spied the jagged rocks,
like razors sharp and vicious.
And deep inside, that voice that mocks,
"You were a tad ambitious."

Upon the reef my hopes were dashed
and as I lay there drowning,
"The Conqueror" was sadly smashed,
my parents left a-frowning.
Now up in Heaven with its views
I contemplate my labour -
and wonder why we didn't use
the bridge of Norm, our neighbour.

LINGUISTIC GYMNASTICS

I'm a word person. In my youth I studied English, French and Latin. I rather fancy my skills at deciphering cryptic crosswords and, in fact, any kind of word puzzles. As a teacher I sometimes challenged my classes to find a word in the dictionary that I couldn't spell or define. The following poems have this in common – they all feature some kind of cleverness with language.

Pardon My French

English is a great borrower of words from other languages. This poem highlights just how much we owe to the French. I was going to add helpful notes to explain the terms used here, but hey, I wouldn't want to spoil the fun you'll get from googling the few that you're not familiar with! For some reason, both this poem and 'Pardon My Latin' which follows headed towards the risqué. Oops! Slipped in another French one.

As I was dining à la carte
Awaiting my entrée,
A mademoiselle with joie de vivre
Showed her décolleté.

"Chérie, I cried, *"it's déjà vu!*
I've seen those breasts before.
Do you recall our rendezvous
When we struck up rapport?"

"That pas de deux's a faux pas past,"
She said with some ennui.
"A quick grope down the cul de sac,
A fast fait accompli."

"But now I'm nouveau riche," I quipped,
"A famous raconteur.
I'm avant-garde, a bon vivant,
I 'ave my own chauffeur.

My concierge's uniform's
The height of haute couture.
When I get pissed upon the piste
It's champagne, that's for sure.

For breakfast I have crêpes suzettes,
For dinner crême brulé.
Will you attend my small soirée,
Répondez s'il vous plaît.

Your skin is sweet café au lait,
And, oh, your derrière!
Cherchez la femme's my raison d'être
There's no more laissez faire."

Money speaks - a cliché, but
It proved the coup de grace,
For as we smooched en route to home
She offered no impasse.

And now dénouement to my tale,
At my place (or Chez Moi)
Where my fiancée waited
For risqué ménage à trois!

Pardon My Latin

Second verse, same as the first! My father wanted me to take Latin because he thought it was an important step towards a potentially profitable career as a pharmacist. I didn't have the heart to tell him that to take Latin, I would have to drop chemistry!

A mental health day is a **sine qua non**
If your **status quo** needs improving upon.
So, brush up your Latinate phrases **et cetera**
As my **alter ego** makes you feel so much betterer!

Mater and **Pater** were gone for the day
Carpe diem I thought, it is my time to play.
I called up my girlfriend; **verbatim** I cite,
"Don't be **in absentia**, I need you tonight."

"I've been working **ad nauseam**, I'm **non compos mentis**.
Please come and spend time in my **loco parentis**.
In vino veritas sounds rather wise
Bring wine then for truth; **tempus fugit!** (time flies!).

Some perfumed oils too may come in rather handy;
Full body massage's my **modus operandi**.
I promise today you'll be my **magnum opus**.
Bring honey, bring grapes and some wee pills to dope us.

Well my plan was **ad hoc** but we soon had a **quorum**
Our **agenda** could fill up the next Penthouse Forum.
Attempting to prove that delight's had in tandem
We tried our **vice versa**, **quod erat demonstrandum**.

We settled *in situ*, no-one could disrupt us;
The last thing we wanted *coitus interruptus*.
Much pleasure *per capita*, more if *pro rata;*
Such tricks should be listed as *desiderata*.

Festina lente, she said, being sneaky.
Too late, I'd already *veni, vidi, vici!*
"*Mea culpa*," I cried. "It's my fault, so *ergo,*
I offer my hand for a quick *quid pro quo*."

I soon had my mitts on a *bona fide* squirmer;
Such joy seldom seen while on our *terra firma!*
Per ardua ad astra, *habeas corpus*, what a time,
No *alias*, no *alibi*, no *prima facie* crime.

Now that may seem *non sequitur*, illogical *per se;*
De facto is, *post coitem*, I don't know what to say.
Re more events that glorious day, there's just *silencium*,
From Descartes to *vox populi*, "*Copulo ergo sum!*"

Abie See De Flim-Flam

This and the following three poems are examples of a form known as Abecedarian. The poems have twenty-six lines, each beginning with one letter of the alphabet. See if you can spot the references to literary personalities and their works here.

Abracadabra and alakazam!
Badjelly's brewing up green eggs and ham.
Contemporaneous colleagues of Carroll
Demonstrably drifted down-snark in a barrel.
Extraterrestrial extravaganzas
Frabjously flitted through each of my stanzas.
Gilbert grew gobbledegook with decorum;
Higgledy-piggledy, high cockalorum.

Isabel et a bear incomprehensibly,
Jawed it like Jabberwock sanely and sensibly.
Kipling and Kafka could kibosh the butterflies;
Lennon flew Lear-jets through marmalade skies.
Milligan's ill again. Mulligatawny
Nourished the neighbour Hood, burly or scrawny.
Oh, what a flibbertegibbet or flummery,
Pam Ayres is wintry or springy or summery.
Quasi-quixotically, using legerdemain
Rambunctious river-rats never the Twain.
Sweet serendipity, Service and Sam Magee
Ta-ra-ra boom de ay, fiddle dee dee.
Un petit, d'un petit, s'etonne aux Halles;
Verily, merrily, Queen of the Ball.
Whereinsoever we widdershins wander,
Xanthippe seeks our resources to squander.
Yikes, what a flim-flam! Thank goodness the end is nigh!
Zippity doo dah! Here's mud in your eye!

A Bestial Compendium

As if the abecedarian form wasn't difficult enough, here I have added the extra challenge of maintaining the initial letter for each word in every line. Do not try this at home!

An average aardvark's ant absorption, annually assessed,
Bewilders baffled Bio boffins, bountifully blessed.
Crocodiles carnivorous can casually consume
Dalmatians, dingoes, dobermans, delivering doggy doom.
Elephants eat eagerly, eschewing etiquette.
Furry, feral foxes feast, forgetting family fret.
Greedy, gourmand, grazing goats go gobbling grass galore.
Happy hippopotami have herein, heretofore,
Ingested (It's incredible!) Iowan indigenes.
Jitterbugging jaguars jump juicy jellybeans.
Ketchup kindles kangaroos, kickstarting king-sized keenness.
Linguini-loving labradors lack legendary leanness.
Marshmellows melted, mayhem make, 'mongst mountain monkey males.
Nibbling nectar nourishes nocturnal nightingales.
Oysters offer ostriches occasional obscurity.
Parrots peck pistachios; pavlovas provide purity.
Quail quiche quickly quenches queasy quaggas' quest.
Rhinos rapidly reduce rainforest's rippling rest.
Sealmeat slightly salted sets seagulls salivating.
Tortoise, turtles, terrapins, think teabags titivating.
Uruguayan ungulates' unparallelled utility-
Veges, vodka, vindaloo verify versatility.
Wildebeest want water-lilies - wilful wanton wheeze!
Xenarthrans xylophilically xerox Xmas-trees.
Yearning, yummy, yellow yams, youthful yaks yell, *"Yippee!"*
Zebras zap zabaglione - zingy, zestful, zippy!

Creed For Modern Living

While the previous two Abecedarians were pure nonsense, this and
the following one have a touch of social commentary about them.
Here I'm revelling in that favourite occupation of the aging
population, aiming a well-deserved smackdown at those under the
age of thirty!

Always check your Facebook page twenty times per day.
Belly, Botox, buttocks, boobs all make a fine display.
Cannabis to crack cocaine's a fine trajectory.
Dabble round in dalliance; eschew monogamy.
Experiment with ecstasy; give crystal meth a try.
Forget the future, live the now; it's happier if you're high.
Games are gory; guns and guts, with violence glorified.
Hug and high five through the day - no chance should be denied.
In parties, pubs, in bars and clubs, drink up till you fall down;
Just remember rehab's costly and your friends can't call around.
Kiss and tell on Instagram, on Twitter or a blog -
Lucky lovers like to know you thought they were a dog.
Music must be loud of course and full of language foul;
Never mind the neighbours - seems that all they do is scowl.
Of morals, you can learn a lot from shows they call reality -
Provocative behaviour plus illusions of normality.
Question everything that stands for moderate sobriety.
Role models should be young and rich, of dubious propriety.
Social networks give you all the news of any value -
Tweets and tags and tit-bits - plenty more they have to tell you.
Unleash the apps on tablet or smart phone and laptop media;
Verify the lessons learned on Bing and Wikipedia.
Words take on new meaning with every hour that passes.
X-Ray vision's obsolete now you have Google Glasses.
Youth is all important; middle-age a concept dirty;
Zero tolerance applies to all who're over thirty.

Dodgy Desiderata

And here just a sneak peek at the criminal mind.

Always have an alibi or, even better, two.
Beware the man who drinks too much, especially if it's you.
Call your lawyer, then your wife. Ask her to bring your bail.
Don't turn your back on Smilin' Jack who runs the whole damn jail.
Expect the unexpected; like a Boy Scout, be prepared.
False bottoms in your cases for those items undeclared.
Guns don't kill but people will; a vest may save your life.
Help out a mate who's locked away by visiting his wife.
Ignorance is no excuse in law you'll often find.
Just a little sweetener can make a cop go blind.
Keep a weather eye out for the snitch who'll spoil your game
Lady Luck's an oxymoron; never trust a dame.
Muscly men with baseball bats deserve your best respecting.
Never mess with Mr Big; kneecaps are worth protecting.
Other people's property's an open invitation.
Protect and serve yourself's the way to wealth accumulation.
Quintessential qualities are quietness and quickness.
Remember to reward yourself; denial's just a sickness.
Some people don't deserve their wealth; here endeth the first lesson.
The only partners that you need are buddies Smith and Wesson.
Unless you want to lose your loot don't bet on cards or dice.
Versatility is good; don't rob the same bank *twice*.
Wear a balaclava when a public place you rob.
Xanax helps if anxious before a tricky job.
You should be grateful God has made so many wealthy fools.
Zealous application is the key to all these rules.

The HOL

What can I say about this one? The original inspiration came from a friend who insisted that he really did once have a website called 'The History of Lecterns.' Somehow, it turned into a riff on TLAs (Three-Letter Acronyms) If that still means diddly-squat to you, just read the damned poem!

HOL I must first say
Is just a simple TLA
If that means SFA to you
Please look it up on the FAQ
FYI it's History
Of Lecterns; you will plainly see
That lecterns had a role to play
In great events of the USA

The Great Depression's squeaky wheel
Was oiled by FDR's New Deal
His trusty lectern, strong and good,
Supported his plan (he knew it would).
J. Edgar Hoover FBI
Thought gangsters all deserved to fry.
His lectern held a lengthy list
Of 'enemies' who'd not be missed.

In West Berlin did JFK
Defy the Soviet might one day.
His lectern (and I swear it's true)
Said *"Ich bin ein Berliner, too."*
MLK with sermons loud
Could stir the passions of a crowd.
The lectern in his back-up team
Was heard to say, *"**WE** have a dream."*

When LBJ went all the way
His speech upon a lectern lay.
"Are we going to Vietnam?"
The lectern muttered, *"Yes I am!"*
When IBM or KFC
Reveal their profits, you will see
A lectern won't be far away;
It's part of corporate DNA

Your classic lectern's AOK
Its wood's approved by FDA
But many a modern VIP
Prefers one made of PVC
If you've a lectern, treat it nice;
With TLC is my advice.
A lectern's death is cruel to see;
How tragic "Lectern RIP"

"WTF," I hear you cry.
"This poet needs an MRI."
No, I'm not high on LSD
I even aced my SAT

In fact at midnight GMT
I shall receive my PhD
My thesis on the HOL
Is OTT, but what the hell?!
They'll show it all on CNN
And ABC at half past ten.
On the stage there's sure to be
A lectern - and that's QED.

Hocus Pocus

For those of you that think sonnets are lovey-dovey things penned by Shakespeare and Shelley, here is one that upsets the norm. See the word 'lovey-dovey' I used above? That's known as a flip-flop word and this poem has one in each line. Following strict sonnet tradition, though, the final couplet has some sound advice!

Advice for razzle-dazzle girl or boy
When faced with hurly-burly of romance:
One should not stoop to mix with hoi-polloi;
Their mumbo-jumbo may induce a trance.

They speak of argy-bargy and the like
And harum-scarum exploits down the street,
Of hanky-panky 'hind the 'shed de bike';
Such tittle-tattle tales they think are sweet.

But you are born of super-duper stock;
Higgledy-piggledy love is not for you.
Such flibbertigibbet games are just a crock
For one whose hoity-toity blood is blue.

Though helter-skelter types may warm your bed,
Do not choose willy-nilly when you wed.

Idiomatic Fanatic

Idiom: a group of words established by usage as having a meaning not deducible from those of the individual words (e.g. over the moon, see the light)

If it were raining cats and dogs,
I might step on a poodle.
If my job were a piece of cake,
I'd make it apple strudel.

If in my bonnet, I'd a bee,
I'd ask him to make honey.
High on the hog is where I'd live,
If only I had money.

Don't look a gift horse in the mouth
Or count your chickens early,
If like a fish you like to drink,
The next day you'll be surly.

Those sleeping dogs, just let them lie;
There's no point waking Rover.
He might bite off more than he'd chew;
You'd really feel done over.

If ev'ry cloud is silver-lined,
I'm taking up prospecting.
I'll work my fingers to the bone,
My just deserts collecting.

I'll batten down the hatches and
I'll keep the wolf at bay.
With lemons I'll make lemonade,
With sunshine I'll make hay.

Good fences make good neighbours and
Let's call a spade a spade.
If monkey business has been done,
Then peanuts will be paid.

On the grapevine I did hear
That beauty's just skin-deep.
If it's got bells and whistles then
That new broom sure can sweep.

Beyond a shadow of a doubt
The best thing since sliced bread
Is finding that a fool rushed in
Where angels feared to tread.

When fortune knocks on doors not mine,
I'll miss the gravy train.
I'd sort the wheat from chaff but it
Would go against the grain

Don't throw a spanner in the works;
I'm out of the equation.
That old fat lady's warming up,
The train has reached the station.

If you have any wild oats left,
Then now's the time to sow 'em.
I know that great minds think alike,
That's why you dig this poem!

Jack

How many different occupations have you had in your lifetime?
Jack (of all trades) has had quite a few, as you can see in the
following poem. He's also quite keen on that commonest of all
humorous devices, the pun!

I could have been an astronaut, but was too starry-eyed;
Then lion-taming tempted, but I didn't have the pride.
I started on a novel once, but soon I lost the plot;
Translating's fun, mais quelle dommage I'm not a polyglot.

I tasted viticulture, *"All sour grapes,"* I have to whine;
Could have made it as an actor if I'd just recalled that line.
Podiatry was a shoo-in until I met defeat;
A copper's job's arresting -- I'm so sad it's got me beat.

I tried out for a butcher, but I didn't make the cut;
I opened 'Doors R Us' but then that opening sadly shut.
I worked at making windows, but I found it was a pain;
A Wall Street broker hired me, but I made a loss a-gain.

A fishing trawler netted me; I knew there'd be a catch;
A dating site employed me; I was fired without a match.
A dairy farmer thought I'd do; alas, no more I've heard;
As cocktail waiters come, I went -- shaken but not stirred.

I tapped a plumber once for work, but knew I shouldn't force it;
Then did a stint at The Royal Mint -- I knew I could out-source it.
A nanny once, I kid you not; a lawyer with no will;
I trained to be a dentist too; I'm sure you know the drill.

I sailed upon a racing yacht, but waved that life goodbye;
I turned to printing T-shirts -- what a job! I'd rather die!
A doctor with no patience, a teacher with no class;
A soccer-playing failure who couldn't get a pass.

A matador with gore galore, I tell you that's no bull;
Librarian? I shelved it, for my CV's far too full.
I could've been a thousand things, but now I'm overjoyed;
There's no way I can lose my job -- I'm flaming unemployed!

MEANDER

Oh, no! now I'll have to try to explain the title for this section which is actually all about male/female relationships. So why 'Meander'? Once defined in a cryptic crossword clue as 'Cockney couple', the word has to be broken down into its parts = Me and 'er. Got it yet? If not, don't ever take up cryptics!

Murphy's Bar

This little dialogue between husband and wife is best read aloud with a partner! His part is in straight text, hers in italics. Have fun as the mood gradually changes through the poem.

O, precious wife, my only love, my sweetheart so sublime,
If it should please your heart, I crave a moment of your time.

O, husband mine, so sweet, so strong, the finest in the land,
My time is yours, as is my heart, your wish is my command.

Most truly said, my turtle-dove; how Providence is kind
To grant this humble person a soulmate so refined.

How may I please you, darling man, the apple of my eye?
Whate'er you seek I'll strive to find or in the seeking die.

'Tis Sunday afternoon, my pet; the game begins at three.
I plan to watch at Murphy's Bar, on his big-screen TV

To Murphy's Bar again, my dear, the third time there this week?
I trust high definition is the only thrill you seek.

O, Buttercup, what can you mean? Your words cut like a knife.
Suspicion's unattractive in the better kind of wife.

You know full well of what I speak; that barmaid known as June.
She's bustin' out all over, and I know you love that tune.

O, Pretty Pumpkin, it's so sad to hear such jealous raving.
You surely know your gorgeous self's the only one I'm craving.

Your words ring false, it's sad to say. To your eternal shame,
As we made love last Tuesday night, you whimpered out her name.

A cry of ecstasy, perhaps, a moan of sheer delight.
"I swoon, I swoon," that's what you heard, as your love gave me flight.

It must have been a short-lived cry, if ecstasy was in it.
As I recall, the whole affair took less than one brief minute.

Impugn my manhood, if you must, but what most makes me grieve
Is the foundless allegation that I would my wife deceive.

Munchausen couldn't lie like you, you slimy little toad.
In all my life I've never heard, of bulldust, such a load.

My Sweet, you wound me with such names, it is a baseless slander.
Such sauce will stick, you jealous cow, to goose as well as gander.

I have it from the horse's mouth, on good authority,
For while you flirt at Murphy's Bar, why, Murphy's here with me!

That gormless clod, that Fenian troll, that lout of little learning?
I see in love, as in fine ale, his taste is not discerning.

I need a man who satisfies, who makes me feel complete.
He's twice the man you ever were; I don't mean just his feet!

You harridan, you vicious hag, your morals run to scarlet.
Why, Murphy's welcome to your wiles, you sleazy, faithless harlot.

The pot may call the kettle black, but hark, is that a car?
Goodbye, my cuckold, don't wait up, I'm off to Murphy's Bar.

Mounting Evidence

Another poem where the mood changes in the course of the
piece. Don't miss the wee pun in the title!

You say you fear I've been untrue,
but no one holds a candle to
yourself. You simply can't be beat....
    They can't compete.

You heard my secretary's got
a bust that's big, a bod that's hot
and acts like she's a bitch in heat,
    Miss Marguerite.

I never touched the girl I swear;
I don't know how her underwear
got in my car behind the seat....
    I did not cheat.

That message on my mobile phone
declaring she was all alone;
would I come by and rub her feet...
    was meant for Pete.

Now that receipt in black and white
revealing that we stayed the night
in Hilton's Honeymooners' Suite....
    That's counterfeit.

And Tom, that Private Eye you hired,
you know he really should be fired.
Those dodgy pics from eighty feet
    are incomplete.

You have a friend who claims she saw
us through a window in the raw.
Your friends, I have to say, my sweet,
    are indiscreet.

Those emails that you say you read
about the joys we found in bed,
the evidence is gone, petite,
    I hit delete.

And now you say you tracked us here,
but look, I am alone, my dear.
You see her butt beneath the sheet?

    Oh, damn! Defeat!

How Do I Love Thee?

-Another sonnet, this time of the Italian or Petrarchan variety. You may recognise the first line which I have borrowed for the occasion from Elizabeth Barrett Browning's sweetly romantic piece to her husband and fellow poet. Our versions diverge drastically after line 1!

How do I love thee? Let me count the ways:
I love thee more than strawberries and cream,
Or cheese on toast grilled to a drizzling dream,
to follow, Danish pastries' sug'ry glaze.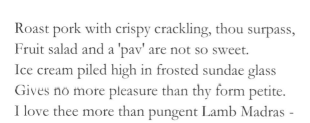
I love thee to a depth that would amaze,
Far more than trout caught fresh from tinkling stream
At dusk, and grilled on charcoal's friendly gleam
Or tea with scones and jam in sweet cafes.

Roast pork with crispy crackling, thou surpass,
Fruit salad and a 'pav' are not so sweet.
Ice cream piled high in frosted sundae glass
Gives no more pleasure than thy form petite.
I love thee more than pungent Lamb Madras -
Excuse me dear, I think I need to eat!

25 Questions for a First Date

I'm imagining one of those speed dating operations. Not that I've ever partaken, but I'm imagining after this barrage of questions, she'll either fall into your arms or run screaming from the room!

This is the only poem in this collection that also appears in my other published book, "Life, Love and Other Disasters," which is available for purchase on Amazon for less than the price of a cup of coffee. Did I already tell you that? Well, did you buy it yet?

Are you losing? Are you winning?
Are you sinned against or sinning?
Do you carry a revolver in your purse?
Is your world a thing of wonder?
Do you bluster, blink and blunder?
Do you greet the dawn with blessings or a curse?

Do you praise the Lord on Sunday,
then forget Him on a Monday?
Is religion just insurance 'gainst the dark?
Are you dying? Are you living?
Are you getting? Are you giving?
Would you rather be the seashell or the shark?

Are you summer, spring or winter?
Run a mile, or just a sprinter?
And when friendship comes a-calling, are you home?
Is it beauty that surrounds you,
or a duty that confounds you?
Are you solid rock or simply frothy foam?

Do your molehills look like mountains?
Do you frolic through the fountains?
Do you love like love is going out of style?
Do you stop to smell the flowers?
Are the seconds, minutes, hours
less important than a sonnet or a smile?

Can I call on you tomorrow?
Are those tears of joy or sorrow?
Is it agony or ecstasy or bliss?
Will you come, my love, a-walking
where the moonlight does the talking?
Will you stop this foolish prattle with a kiss?

Fitting Torture

If you are male and you can empathise with this tale then you have my most profound commiserations! No breaks in this one – I think it's fun if you attempt to read it all in one breath! Go!

There's one thing that can truly vex
about the lovely fairer sex:
they cannot pass a clothing shop
without a sudden reckless stop-
no brake or turn light, understand?
No slowing down or wave of hand.
"I'll just be one (or two, or five)
minutes." That's the kind of jive
they try to feed you, though you know
they'll prob'ly be an hour or so,
and what are you supposed to do
while she goes *'Um'* and *'Ah'* and *'Ooh'*?
The boredom's grand, it's continental;
half an hour can drive you mental,
and then she grabs a pile of stuff
ten skirts, ten tops, is that enough
to try on in the fitting room?
I'd rather rest inside my tomb;
it's cruel, unfair, it's inhumane.
Outside I faithfully remain
while snarling dragon ladies glare
and wonder why I'm lurking there.
I know their thoughts, I read their minds,
"He wants to look at our behinds!
See how his evil eyelid flickers;
he wants to watch us in our knickers!"
SECURITY, DEPARTMENT THREE
A LOITERER IN THE LINGERIE!!

But wait, the worst is yet to come;
"How do I look?" and *"Does my bum*
look huge in this or vast, immense?"
Oh, come on now, I'm not that dense!
The only answer that's worth phrasing
is, *"Oh, My God, you look amazing!"*
"I'm not quite sure," she coos and then...
... back to the fitting room again!
The only thing that can console
is when I spot a kindred soul;
the glassy eye, the hangdog look,
the sense that fortune long forsook.
Together we commiserate
and plot revenge against each mate.
At last the torture session's ended.
Please God may it seem I've pretended
enjoyment of this shopping spree.
"My sweet, I pray, a word with thee;
Together with my new friend Rolf,
Tomorrow I'll be playing golf!"

LIMERICKS

According to well-known advice:

The Limerick packs laughs anatomical
In space that is quite economical.
   But the good ones I've seen
   So seldom are clean
And the clean ones so seldom are comical.

*Here are some of both varieties so you can evaluate the theory
for yourself.*

Camelot Carry-On

It was his wand that did the trick.

With Merlin, the wise old magician,
Queen Guinevere lost inhibition.
   According to fable,
   Upon the Round Table,
His magic spell came to fruition.

Merry on the Ferry

A different sort of cautionary tale...

When crossing to Calais by ferry,
A maiden imbibed too much sherry.
   When she woke up in France,
   She was minus her pants.
Her bra, her respect and her cherry.

Three Bright Sparks

And finally, three more candidates for the Darwin awards...

Photographer Inge de Bruin
Risked danger for art -- 'twas her ruin.
   One day off Majorca
   She swam with the Orca
Her last shots were great teeth a-chewin'.

~~"~~"~~"~~

Mad Mike, a mechanic from Twickenham
Loved cars -- his passion to quicken 'em.
   Fine-tuning emulsion
   Achieved jet-propulsion -
Today in his grave they are stickin' 'im.

~~"~~"~~"~~

A physicist-mathematician
Made constant excitement his mission
   Snorted uranium
   Into his cranium
And Boom! he achieved nuclear fission

SHEER NONSENSE

In English class we may be asked to analyse poems for their diction, their form and their all-important theme, but sometimes poems don't have anything important to say, they are just for fun. I've been accused at times of channelling Lewis Carroll (one of my heroes) or even Dr Seuss. See what you think.

Yellow Wellies

Perhaps I had been swilling a little too much 'Tofu Tea' when I penned this one. Watch out for flatulent flamingos, everyone!

When I wore my yellow wellies
  and went down to Aunty Sally's,
    she was drinking Tofu tea with Cousin Bob.
Seems a walrus with pink flippers
  had eloped with Suzy's slippers
    and run off to Timbuktu to find a job.

Then a pack of leaping llamas
  in their polka-dot pyjamas
    sang a lullaby in shades of pearly pink.
Down in Crazy Horse's teepee
  all the eskimos grew sleepy
    and the flatulent flamingo took to drink.

Though the details may be murky,
  I remember that a turkey
    blew the whistle on Thanksgiving to our host.
There were Crêpes Louisiana
  and a bear in a bandana
    found Bill Hickok taking potshots at a ghost.

Then a jaunty little fella
  and a geisha with umbrella
    whispered, *"Rosencrantz and Guildenstern are dead."*
Life is fleeting, little sweeting;
  are we winning or retreating
    or just waking up with cake-crumbs in the bed?

The Sandwich-Oyster Platter

Perhaps no coincidence that this has the rhyme scheme and metre and even the setting of Lewis Carroll's "The Walrus and the Carpenter."

An oyster and a sandwich-man, while strolling on the beach,
Were pleased to find the pears divine, with mango, quince and peach.
"If we could only pluck," they cried, *"fresh truffles from the sky,*
'Tis certain, in an instant, our restaurant would fly."

The sandwich-man shook out the sand that gathered in his slices;
"Why we could charge the world at large the most delicious prices.
I'd like to have a menu that was three or four feet high.
I have a hunch that folk would lunch on pork and pecan pie."

"Upon my shell, I know it well," the oyster gravely stated,
"Though did you know that escargots are vastly over-rated?
But bouillabaisse with pickled plaice and dugong fricasseed
And crepes suzette, the best you've et, and fragrant fennel mead..."

In great excitement, thus, the pair their prospects reconnoitred;
Alas they failed to notice that for far too long they'd loitered.
The tide rushed in with whooshing din and drowned their foody chatter -
Just like my rhyme, here ends their time - the Sandwich-Oyster Platter.

How to Befriend a Platypus

I once had a chance to see a platypus in the wild. Such a strangely beautiful creature obviously deserves the homage of a very strange poem.

Should you ride on a bus with the proud Platypus,
Who's a strange and implacable beast,
You may give him a stare like a bathroom chair -
Will it bother him? Not in the least!

You may tap on his toes with a green garden hose,
You may comb all his hair with a rake,
Yet he'll bid you, *"Good day,"* in a nonchalant way,
Just as if it were all a mistake.

If you pull on the bell; if the driver should yell,
And the passengers leap to their feet,
You may see in his eyes just a hint of surprise
And you'll know that you've got his bluff beat.

And then if you will simply pay off his bill
And praise his exemplary bearing.
It's certain you'll find he'll have presence of mind
To refrain from all swimming and swearing.

Now just give of your time to compose a wee rhyme
Or cajole him with cockles and cream.
By the very next stop, all reserve he will drop
And invite you back home to his stream.

Moonshine

*Pets are great, aren't they? They can be a little demanding at times, though. I remember the origin of this piece – cats and dogs either very hungry or very keen to go out or come in. That accounts for **Wow-Wow** and **Grizzly**; I have no idea where all the other characters came from!*

Wow-Wow and Grizzly and Grumpy and Fat
All lived on the moon in a wee council flat,
With a moon-dog, an alien, Grumpy's old mother,
A whatchamacallit, a something-or-other
A wizard, a warlock, a pirate or two
And a wrinkled old warthog escaped from the zoo.

They shared a big breakfast with most fulsome mirth
In the light of the fragile and faraway Earth.
The moon-eggs were scrambled, the moon-bacon fried;
Said the warthog, *"I'm fuller than Frankenstein's bride.*
I once dined on quince with a runcible spoon,
But nothing beats blueberry pie on the moon."

The queue for the bathroom stretched far down the hall;
The moon-dog insisted on chasing his ball.
The warlock grew tetchy, the pirates grew terse,
The wizard froze Grumpy's old Mum with a curse.
The whatchamacallit shed crocodile tears,
The alien wiggled all five of his ears.

Then Wow-Wow grew maudlin and started to weep;
"Oh where, " he cried, *"where will these critters all sleep?"*
But Grizzly soon cheered him, *"You worry too soon;*
I know for a fact there's no night on the moon."
"Aha!" cried the pirates, *"You think you're so clever!*
We come from the dark side where night lasts forever."

Soon something-or-other got into a spat
With warthog and moon-dog and Grumpy and Fat,
While Grumpy's old mother awoke from her trance
And shyly invited the wizard to dance.
In a flash the whole household was paired off in threes
And they tangoed till twilight 'neath tropical trees.

… and for the Defence

I have a wonderful book of sonnets by American poet Sara Henderson Hay. Each of the poems provides a fresh perspective on a fairy tale or nursery rhyme. For example the third little pig, the smart one, voices his disdain for his not so smart brothers who got eaten and one of the children of the old woman who lived in a shoe now hangs around in alleyways waiting to accost and murder anyone who reminds him of his abusive mother. I guess this piece attempts the same thing, giving the wolf a chance to defend himself.

I blame that little minx -- you know the one
with cutesy cape and hood of brightest red.
The basket that she carried, from her Mum,
was for her Grandma -- least that's what she said.

And so I ran ahead to pave the way,
prepare ol' Granny for her coming guest,
but found the cottage empty. Now, I pray
you'll understand, I felt the need to rest.

The drama that unfolded..... well, you've heard.
That business with the eyes, the ears, the teeth,
was so exaggerated, quite absurd.
Though I have wolfish features, look beneath.

That woodsman fell on his own lethal axe;
and Little Red and Grandma? Heart attacks!

Behind the Door

Oh yes, this seems all too real

Behind the door's a pile of dust;
I'll vacuum soon; I must! I must!
But first I'll pick up that old sock
So that my Hoover pipe won't block.

And look, there are my third-best knickers!
How did they get....? Oh! (quietly snickers)
Those keys that vanished last September -
Changed all the locks, as I remember.

A gas bill, seven lollipops,
With tiny teeth-marks on their tops;
A Christmas card from cousin Sue -
My God, it's post-marked Kathmandu!

A dozen pens, some paper-clips
And half a pack of PG Tips,
A fax machine, still in its carton,
Some records.... Oooh! They're Dolly Parton!

That spider's web, strong as a net -
And there's the blighter spinning yet.
What's that he's trapped? looks like a whippet;
I'll need hedge clippers just to snip it.

Could that be Elvis under there?
And Michael Jackson, by the hair?
A pyramid, some standing stones,
Lord Lucan holding Shergar's bones.

Jimmy Hoffa, Harold Holt,
Davy Crockett, Samuel Colt,
The Queen of Hearts, the King of Spain,
Amelia Earhart in her plane.

Harry Potter's black-rimmed specs,
Uh-oh, Tyrannosaurus Rex...
Quick, slam the door, let's not go near;
Perhaps I'll clean that room next year!

From Sir With Love

Every teacher has had this feeling.

I remember sharing his poem with one of my classes and they commented that none of their names appeared in it. It just took a little tweak to insert them, which tickled them immensely. How are you doing, Woree State High School?

My job is teaching children who seldom want to learn;
They give me flak, a panic attack, a headache and heartburn.
I don't mean little rug-rats, I mean great lumbering louts;
No wonder every morning I have malingering doubts!

They push and shove and quarrel, and flash malicious looks,
And half of them don't come prepared with stationery or books.
The kids all sit there listening to their Ipods or the like,
Or chatting on their mobile phones to Sam and Chris and Mike.

That new kid fresh from juvie's having trouble sitting still,
And Casey's teasing Anna, who takes it out on Jill,
While Jill won't sit with Amber, 'cos she's got a crush on Bruce;
This class is like a battleground, I'd like to call a truce!

Some kids just need a cuddle, and some I'd like to flay;
Too bad I can't do either, or I'd soon be on my way.
Like Pavlov's dogs I'm waiting for the ringing of the bell,
The signal of salvation, the escape from daily Hell.

The hours seem rather cushy and the holidays are great,
But tons of bloody marking keeps me sitting up till late.
The principal keeps adding another task to do;
I must be a pastoral carer and a nurse and nanny too!

I never get a lunchtime, there's barely time to pee,
As I seek elusive smokers who lurk behind a tree.
There's meetings every other day and most go on for ages,
Professional reading also, of several thousand pages.

Community involvement is a brand new expectation;
Oh, my brain is getting tired I could do with a vacation.
My jaw goes slack, my eyelids droop, I start to swoon and squirm;
When will this day be over, the first one of the term?!

Grandpa, You're Dreaming Again

This will be me in a few years. Dreams are free, aren't they?

I'd like to tread them railway lines
Until they bloomin' vanish;
And then I'd toast my love at dawn
In French, or maybe Spanish.

I'd like to kick the winning goal
At Twickenham or Wembley,
Or woo the war-mad world to peace
At UN's grand Assembly.

I'd like to pilot rocket-ships
That dance among the stars;
Discover long-lost relatives
On Jupiter and Mars.

I'd like to see my name in lights,
Give Hollywood a whirl;
I could play the sneering villain
Or the bloke who gets the girl.

Well, I'd better get my skates on
Cos I'm nearly ninety-one
And the footy's on the telly -
I can't start till *that* is done!

Lost Youth

I believe I have invented a totally new verse form with this piece. I have named it the dipstych (pronounced 'DIP-Stick') It was developed from an ancient Mongolian verse form practised by yak-herders in the frozen wastes of outer Mongolia to while away the boredom of long, bitter winters. The classic begins:
's a fac', my yak
He is stronger.
His coat, take a vote.
Is longer.

I'll conduct classes on how to write this new form. Contact PoetForHire and I'll let you know how to pay the $5,000 fee.

Synapses getting lapses?
    Exercise 'em.
Brood got a 'tude?
    Chastise 'em.

Prob wit' your mob?
    Disinherit.
No show that you know
    Got merit?

Bones causing groans?
    Hear 'em creaking.
Pain like your brain
    May be leaking?

Young folk a joke,
    Music blaring.
Crazy hats and those tats
    They're all wearing.

Lost specs a hex?
   Attach 'em
Pursuit of the cute?
   Can't catch 'em.

In hock to your doc?
   Try suing.
Oh, please, MPs
   What you doing?

Pee frequently?
   Tie a knot in it.
Can't read what your feed
   Has got in it.

Sprinkle when you tinkle?
   Aim straighter.
Can't recall sex at all?
   A spectator.

Bed at eight seems late,
   Seven's better.
Old flame, whatsername?
   Forget 'er.

A pox on the box
   Not worth viewing.
Can't tell what the hell
   They are doing.

Lost youth it's the truth
   Can't defy it.
Don't rage at your age
   Just deny it.

Nicholas the Happy Nicker

Light-hearted and light-fingered.

One Nicholas "Nickers" Bartholomew Miles
Is a fellow who's highly gregarious,
But this charming young chap with a face wreathed in smiles
Has a talent for actions nefarious.

Ev'ry night he will peck his sweet wife on the cheek
And tickle his kids till they're gurgling;
On his back there's a sack of utensils unique,
And he's off for a good night of burgling.

'Neath a smuggler's moon he will steal through the town
In a search for a target particular.
He'll disarm the alarm, he'll climb up and climb down,
Though the high walls are quite perpendicular.

Now Nicholas knows that he'll never be nabbed
By an ordinary copper or bobby,
For the pearls he's purloined and the gold that he's grabbed
Are the fruits of much more than a hobby.

It's a calling, a passion, a mission, an art,
Nothing less than a true avocation;
And our hero has thievery deep in his heart;
It's his only careeer aspiration.

His Dad was a robber, his grandfather too,
Two uncles, three nephews, ten cousins.
In his family tree, twenty pirates all grew,
There were crooks, owls and thieves by the dozens;

While a few of the crew, to add meat to the stew,
Were blessed with much higher ambitions;
A comp'ny director, the chief taxman too,
Plus a p'liceman and five politicians.

But our Nickers surpassed all those crooks we are told
In his acumen and his ability
To sniff out a big stash of diamonds or gold,
And with safe-cracking skills and agility.

So if thievery were an Olympic event,
Erased of the shame and the odium,
It's our pick that young Nick to the Games would be sent
And would soon stand on top of the podium.

Pythagoras' Dream

Occasionally when short of inspiration I recycle an old joke, giving it new life by versifying it. This is one of those. I hope you remember Mr P's Theorem. You'll need it for the punchline.

In dream I gazed in wonder where
A pantheon of chiefs I saw;
Geronimo with skin of bear
Appeared and introduced his squaw,
A tawny beauty, meek and mild
Accompanied by a young boy-child.

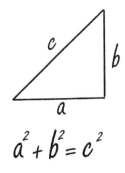

Next, Sitting Bull and wife appeared,
With skin of elk their girl-child wrapped,
The chief whom Custer's soldiers feared
By all those present cheered and clapped.
Apache bold and mighty Sioux
Stood side by side, their families too.

I'm sure you know Longfellow told
Of Hiawatha and his bride;
Before my eyes the hero bold
With Minnehaha by his side.
A hippo hide their choice of skins
To warm their boy- and girl-child twins.

I pondered long on this event,
Some lesson clear I sought to gain,
Till I discovered what it meant;
My final couplet will explain.
The squaw on Hippopot provides
The sum of squaws on other hides!

Redistribution

I remember that a few of the lines for this flashed into my brain while I was walking the dog one evening. Alas, it is not a sure-fire method or Womble would be the fittest dog in the country.

Isn't it curious some are penurious
While others have money to burn
The only solution is re-distribution
There's a lesson from history to learn.

In Sherwood so green Robin Hood could be seen
Relieving the rich of their treasure;
Then Robin the Bold shared the plunder, we're told,
With the poor who awaited his pleasure.

In the highwayman game, Dick Turpin found fame;
Black Bess was his steed strong and speedy.
With his pistols in hand, he ravaged the land,
Then distributed loot to the needy.

Butch Cassidy could, so it seems, have been good,
As portrayed in 'that' film by Paul Newman.
Though raindrops were falling, he followed his calling
Though a robber, he still remained human.

Engels and Marx were a pair of bright sparks
Who wanted to change the whole system.
Their manifest' stealthy, quite panicked the wealthy
While the working class just coulda kissed 'em.

If I could just find such a criminal mind
Whose thiev'ry achieved virtuosity,
There's no use denying I'd soon be applying
To sample his great generosity.

Wake Me When It's Over

Hmmm… this one's a bit dated, isn't it? I've fitted it in because I like the alliteration and the whole overdone nature of royal weddings still drives me crazy!

Will you wemember where you were when Wills and Kate were wed?
Or shall this silly saga sail six sheets above your head?
And 'ave you all arranged your 'ats, an asset at the Abbey?
Foregone fried food, foresworn fine ale so you're not fat and flabby?

Now ninety nuptial nincumpoops are nixing nightly news,
While raging royalists rave about romantic rendezvous.
 VIP's all vainly vie for invites valued high,
Did they all do this doltish dance for Charles and Lady Di?

A pack of paparazzi prey upon the pair of lovers
Like leeches lusting for a lapse to lighten lurid covers
As gatherings of guests garb up in gowns and glam and glitter
It's time to turn the telly off and ditto text and Twitter

I'm sick of kitsch and cake and Kate, of cabbages and kings
I'll threaten to throw up unless they think of other things.
My muddled mind may make me miss this marriage of the year,
But forty fousand follow-ups will fill me in I fear!

TALL TALES

This final section is devoted to tales where hyperbole takes over and any semblance of real life flies right out the window. Baron Munchausen, a fictional character, although based on a real person, is the king of tall tales. He has already gained a mention in an earlier poem in this book.

I remember one story where he had no shot left for his gun, but still managed to kill seven ducks by using a precious gem as a bullet. The ducks flew in a line and the shot pierced the first six. The seventh was also shot but the gem remained in its body to be retrieved by the noble sportsman!

All that you the reader need to do is sit back, engage your imagination and your sense of fun and enjoy the far-fetched action.

Fingery Lickits

I clearly had some fun with the narrative voice in this one and spellcheck just went ballistic! I don't know where this Cajun, patois, dialect, lingo came from, but it certainly gives the story a boost. Any difficulty you have comprehending should vanish if you simply read this aloud; perhaps not in public if you wish to avoid being mistaken for a crazy person.

Yumpin' Yehosophats! Yimminy Crickets!
Mammy be bakin' up fingery lickits.
Dere in de kitchen she's whippin' an' stirrin'
Dose sweet-smellin' mixtures is bubblin' an' whirrin'.
Sugary, buttery, chocolatey fluff
Wiv chopped nuts and cherries an' uvver great stuff.
Now free dozen eggs and a barrel of flour,
Den let it all brew for free quarters an hour.

We'll prob'ly need pow'r from de national grid
Cos we stoke up de stove til he's flippin' his lid.
An' jes' when it looks like de whole fing's explodin'
We open de door an' we caref'ly start loadin.
One tray for me pappy and one for me mam
Den one for Wee Willy an' fat Uncle Sam
A tray for de neighbours, a tray for de dog,
An' one for ol' Benjamin, sleeps in a log.
A pile for de preacher, a pack for de Queen,
An' a mess for de gypsies who live on de green.

Dat ol' oven's groanin', how long can he last?
Dere's twenny more trays an' we shove 'em in fast.
By now de whole neighbourhood's sniffin' an' slaverin'
Dey's getting' strong whiffs of aromas an' flavourin'
Norf-east by westerly, dat's where it's headin',
More pow'rful dan wildcats dat sweet smell is spreadin'.

Souf to Alaska an' Norf-east to Rome
Wherever dere's hungry folks sittin' at home.
De Pope in his palace, de Queen on 'er frone
Dem President mans wiv dems heads turned to stone;

Chinese an' Japanese more dan are listable
Are lickin' dems lips at the tang irresistible.
Huskies in harness an' cowboys in chaps,
Reindeer an' race-drivers countin' down laps;
Kangaroos, kiwis an' karma battalions,
Hippies wiv flowers an' peace sign medallions;
In fact de whole world and some ETs as well
Are drawn to de source of dat framjumptious smell.

An', meanwhile me mammy is whippin' up cream
Ten buckets she'll do wiv a good head of steam.
Twelve gallons of icin', a hogshead of jam,
Wiv brandy a snifter an' whisky a dram.
De cookin's near finished, my taste buds is droolin',
dey gush wiv a rush, to de floor where dey're poolin'
My heartbeat is poundin', all flimmity-flammity,
When oh what a gastro-catastro-calamity

Me mammy, more sprightly dan lady Godiva,
Slips into dat pond of unsightly saliva.

No wonder she's yellin', no wonder she's frownin',
It's apparent to all she's not wavin' but drownin'.
Now sadly de coastguard ain't nowhere in sight
No lifeguards come rushin' to help wiv 'er plight.
No CPR guru to thump and inflate 'er
No ambulance man with a defibrillator.
So wiv barely a whimper, this marvellous baker
'Ad popped 'er ol' clogs an' gone off to 'er maker.

An' much worse was to come, as king Alfred had learnt,
If yer don't watch yer cakes, den dey's apt to be burnt.
Dere rose a great pillar of smoke from de oven,
More black dan a posse of witches, a coven.
Den a flame flickered out like de tongue of a lizard,
A flurry of sparks, den a storm den a blizzard.
In a matter of minutes a gran' conflagration
'Ad swallered our 'ouse an' de pride of our nation.
Yes me mammy was gone wiv 'er cookbook collection,
No more jammy scones nor no pink-iced confections.
But the tragedy truly I jes' cannot kick it
Is to never again taste a fingery lickit.

Country Justice

Even judges make mistakes.

Where the river runs down, through our small country town -
One school and an ambulance station;
Plus a servo, a pub and place that serves grub -
There's a courthouse of high reputation.

In the field of the law, one Augustus McGraw
Spoke wisely with true erudition.
As the judge in this town he sent many men down
And justified each imposition.

"It's my job," he would say, *"to make criminals pay;"*
His growling voice gritty as gravel.
"In a courtroom of mine, you had best toe the line."
And he'd silence the room with his gavel.

Then one day to his court a young speedster was brought;
Her name was Roberta McGlashan.
She was tall, she was sweet; from her crown to her feet,
She dressed in the latest of fashion.

As she stood 'fore the judge it was hard to begrudge
A tear for this winsome young filly.
"Maybe this time you'll learn," said his Honour, so stern.
"Exceeding the limit was silly."

So, Roberta she sighed, and, *"Your Honour,"* she cried,
And she batted her lashes quite cutely.
Then the buxom young wench smartly bowed to the bench,
Exploiting her assets astutely.

Well, a tear glistened there on her features so fair,
A crystal clear sign of repentance;
Mr Justice McGraw clearly liked what he saw-
He paused before passing his sentence.

"I can see that you've learned, so this case is adjourned.
Come see me for clarification.
When the courtroom is clear, in my rooms over there,
We'll work towards mutual elation."

Well, Roberta and Gus might have settled things thus,
Conjoined in successful class action,
If it weren't for a hitch, just the tiniest glitch
Preventing complete satisfaction.

Soon the two were alone and they'd turned off the phone,
T'was time for full frontal disclosure,
When an obvious knob proved Roberta was Rob
And prone to indecent exposure.

Rank Frank Robs a Bank

How many rhyming words can you think of that end with the sound of the letter K? You're about to find out in this piece of silliness.

Now there's some folk cain't take a joke;
Their faces just look blank
They'd rather croak than hear one spoke,
Or play a silly prank.

Take my friend, Jock; he can't unlock
A smidgen of a smirk.
Though you may mock, he's like a rock;
His smiler just don't work.

Just like a monk, Jock's fun-bone's shrunk;
He's never run amok.
Though he's no punk, he keeps a skunk;
He calls him 'In' for luck.

One grey day dank, Jock's at the bank;
He toils behind his desk;
When in bursts Frank, his hair all lank,
In costume quite grotesque.

He wore a mac and wig of black,
He had a fish-net mask.
A gunny-sack was on his back
To tote the cash he'd ask.

The tellers took a fleeting look;
They spied his shiny Glock
And slung their hook, their posts forsook,
Except me old mate, Jock.

See, Jock showed pluck, he had no truck
With bandits of this ilk.
"Your actions suck, you silly schmuck!"
He cried, then moved like silk.

Now Jock was slick, he pulled a trick,
He didn't stop to think.
With one smooth flick, he hurled In quick,
Before poor Frank could think.

This simple act showed what Frank lacked;
Capacity to duck.
Upon impact, it is a fact
That he was thunderstruck.

It's hard to fake the smell skunks make,
It sure can make you puke.
A putrid lake of pong opaque,
It felled Frank like a nuke.

So let's not knock my good friend, Jock;
Whoever would have thinked?
Oh what a shock, no more the rock,
He acts upon In-stinked.

Dead Duck

Another of the recycled joke variety.

A duck was Robert's favourite pet;
They paid a visit to the vet,
And, *"I'm afraid,"* the good man said,
"Your duck's not poorly; he's quite dead!"

Bob cried, *"Oh, no! It can't be so.*
He swam and quacked one hour ago.
There must be something to be done,
Some other test that you could run."

The vet said that he had a minion
Who could give her esteemed opinion.
How Robert was amazed at that;
The colleague was a pussy-cat!

The feline doctor poked and purred
As she examined the 'sick' bird,
Then shook her head and gave a sigh;
No need to ask the reason why.

But Bob could still not be consoled,
Excessive grief had made him bold.
He wailed, *"I really must be sure*
That there's no hope of earthly cure."

So then the vet just trotted out
The one he said would leave no doubt,
And even stranger than before,
This expert was a labrador!

The dog soon saw he'd have no luck
At rousing the departed duck;
He gave his golden head a shake
Confirming there was no mistake.

And as poor Bob was grieving still,
He was presented with the bill.
"What's this?" cried Bob. *"Don't be absurd!"*
"Five hundred bucks for one dead bird!"

"I feel your pain," the vet replied,
*"And though it hurts me deep inside,
My fee I waived, but then you bought
The CAT scan and the LAB Report!"*

Pirates Aplenty

And this is simply a piece of buccaneering fun!

Here's pirates a-plenty, all singing a shanty,
There's Peg-Leg and Piggy and Pippin and Paul.
"Ah Hoy!" cries the captain, whose grammar is scanty,
"You 'scallions ain't makin' not no sense at all!"

You think that they hear him? You think that they're list'ning?
Not Funky, not Monkey, not Punky, not Pete.
They're scaling the rigging, they're brawling, they're jigging;
There's not a man jack of 'em firm on his feet.

The captain grows cranky, he pulls out his hanky,
He swishes his cutlass and swivels his hook.
"Oi, Snippy and Lippy! Oi, Limpy and Lanky!
You knucklehead buccaneers, we need a cook!"

"There's tall ships to plunder; we'll tear 'em asunder,
We'll scaramouche all of their diamonds and gold.
We'll dance at our leisure on mountains of treasure;
With silvery salvers we'll stock up our hold."

"We're stuck in this harbour, we've been to the Barber,
We've drunk all the rum and we've kissed all the girls.
I'se begging, I'se pleading, we'se all need a feeding
'Fore setting to sea after rubies and pearls."

"Is there none of this rabble can dredge up a drabble
Or sauté a seagull to serve in a pie?
We just cannot risk it on weevil and biscuit,
We've got to find someone to frazzle and fry."

The crew grow uneasy and quiv'ry and queasy;
They shuffle and shamble and stare at the deck,
When out from the rear, rings a voice loud and clear,
"I'll do it. I'll do it. I'll do it, by heck!"

'Tis cabin-boy Gramsay, a meek little lambsy,
You'd never think butter would melt in his mouth.
"You men all mariney deserve haute cuisiney,
And I'll serve it up, take me north, take me south."

"Want blowfish and glowfish and kelp a la mode?
A hurtle of turtle dished up in its case?
I'll cook 'em right now with the hole and its toad,
And follow it up with a fine bouillebaisse!"

"Seafowl au gratin and walrus flambe,
Octopus pickled, or baked and en croute,
Chowder and chutney and moray mornay,
With lashings of lobster and oysters to boot."

The captain's bedazzled, the crew are ecstatic
And Polygon Parrot gives out a loud shriek.
The cheering for Gramsay's both loud and emphatic.
These brigands, it seems, will be hoarse for a week.

They haul in the hawsers, they pull up the plank,
Then hoist Jolly Roger to top of the mast.
The next time they land here it's off to the bank;
The Pirate Ship Gourmand is sailing at last.

Trouble at the Pole

Did you by any chance receive this book as a Christmas gift?
Better have a Christmassy piece, then!

When Santa got pulled over by a booze-bus, late one night,
They took away his licence so he couldn't make his flight.
Oh, what a panic at the pole, the elves were in hysterics,
Till Mrs Sandy Claus cried out, *"No need for atmospherics!"*

"The task can't be so difficult, he's done it rolling drunk.
Let no one shirk, just get to work, load good stuff, not the junk.
Prioritise and organise; his system was pathetic.
Make sure you stack from front to back, and make it alphabetic."

You reindeer, get your antlers on. Stand over here in rows.
And, Rudolph, I'm half blinded -- can you dim that bloody nose!?"
The elves were swayed, they all obeyed; the reindeer did the same,
Though in the herd, a word was heard -- perhaps 'twas Blitzen's
name.

The sleigh was packed, each parcel tracked, all ready for the trip.
God help the elf who slipped or slacked when Sandy cracked the
whip!
The reindeer too, like wind they flew. Whoever would have guessed
it?
She had a list, no house was missed, cos Sandy GPS'd it.

Some things were changed or re-arranged -- seems Sandy was too snooty
To clamber down a chimney lest she got her costume sooty.
No milk or cookies were consumed, no wine, no beer, no whisky -
The designated driver deemed they'd make her fat or frisky.

Each good child matched, each gift dispatched, and all in record time;
Around the world and back they twirled, to home in polar clime,
Where Santa had been very bad, his day off celebrated -
The elves and he, quite selfishly, were all inebriated.

Well, Mrs Claus, she did not pause, her voice grew harsh and squawky,
And to this day there's some folk say they heard her in Milwaukee!
"You drunken slob, I've done your job, and saved the family bacon,
And if you think that's cause to drink, you're very much mistaken."

I'll want, of course, a quick divorce -- no changing my decision.
You can't dispute my legal suit for property division.
I'm taking all the reindeer herd, I'll sell their hide for chamois;
*And you can keep **this** freezing heap -- I'm moving to Miami!"*

MERRY  CHRISTMAS

Index of titles

Index of First Lines

ABOUT THE AUTHOR

Steve Herbert is a Kiwi. Like most of his kind, he is a laid-back fellow, fond of a joke, who enjoys nothing more than watching the all-conquering All Blacks demolish the latest pretender to the Rugby's throne. On TV of course. Actually going to the game would require more effort than seems worthwhile; and money, which poets don't generally have.

A teacher for most of his life, he has nurtured budding minds in rural New Zealand, in the hustle and bustle of Singapore, and in the tropical heat of Australia's Far North Queensland. Now back in his homeland, he attempts to maintain a run-down little place in the wilds of Northland – that's the pointy bit at the top of the North Island. Preventing him from writing quite as much as he would like are two cats, a dog, three goats and five chickens. And the wife, of course, who seems to see some sort of virtue in having clothes on her back and food on the table.

Steve Herbert has published one previous book of poetry, much more serious than this one. It is called *Life, Love and Other Disasters* and is available for purchase on Amazon.

He may be contacted via email at poetforhire@xtra.co.nz or you can find more of his poetry and other snippets of literary interest on his facebook page Facebook.com/Poetforhire.nz

Made in the USA
Las Vegas, NV
28 December 2021

39689851R00069